Freemasons

The Hidden History of Freemasonry in the Last 100 Years

Conrad Bauer

MAPLEWOOD
– PUBLISHING –

Contents

Introduction

In their three centuries of official existence, Freemasons have been routinely praised and despised, regularly cheered and derided. Some believe that they are a fraternal organization that promotes leadership and good character, while others are convinced that they are a secretive cabal hell-bent on world domination. Mason-backed organizations such as the Shriners are praised for their charitable giving, while other lodges are held in contempt for their secretiveness.

When it comes to stark dichotomies such as this, the argument to moderation would indicate that the truth lies somewhere in between. Well, fallacious as that argument is, Freemasonry would still be a riveting tale even if it *did* fall neatly between both sides of the equation!

In this book we will explore the last 100 years of Freemasonry, as well as the larger implications of Masonic influence and practice. We will also discuss Masonry's latest trends and probable future trajectory. So, if you don't know already—read this book to learn the full story of what really goes on in that quiet, nondescript little lodge on the corner! Because despite what your grandfather may have told you, there is more going on than card games, pancakes and fish fries! Here, in one concise chronological timeline, discover the last 100 years of Freemasonry!

The Roots of Freemasonry

The roots of Freemasonry have always been shrouded in mystery, but many authorities trace them all the way back to the siege of Jerusalem in 1099 AD. This siege, waged by European invaders against Arab defenders, was set in motion by the Pope's call for a Crusade against the Muslim powers then occupying the Holy Land. The reasons behind this sudden Christian Crusade against Islam have long been hotly debated, and the narrative has frequently changed over the centuries in order to match the political aims of those telling the story.

To cut through some of the spin-doctoring and get a better understanding of this complicated backdrop, let's just lay out the bare-bones facts. First, you have to consider how many times the Holy Land has actually changed hands. The Jews controlled the region from about 1000 BC to 70 AD, after which it was the Roman Empire's turn. The Romans forcibly expelled most Jews after laying waste to Jerusalem and burning down the centerpiece of Judaism, the holy Temple. At this point in history, the Romans were pagans and not much interested in the Jews' monotheistic religion or the relics they left behind. This changed after a Roman Emperor named Constantine came to power in 306 AD. Constantine, initially a pagan himself, eventually turned toward Christianity, and with his conversion the entire Roman Empire followed suit.

In one of the most remarkable reversals in history, an Empire that had once fed Christians to the lions for entertainment in its arenas and coliseums became Christian itself. This revived interest in the Empire's Eastern frontier—the Middle Eastern lands Jesus had once walked—and this led to the building of new churches and infrastructure in these previously abandoned backwaters. In the coming centuries, however, the ancient superpower of Roman civilization began to wane, and as it weakened it became increasingly hard for it to protect its far-flung borders.

By 600 AD the rise of a powerful new religion called Islam forced the Roman Catholics from the Middle East. These erstwhile Christian lands were forcibly converted to Islam and placed under direct Muslim control. This was the status quo for the next few centuries, until in the year 1095 Pope Urban II issued a call to arms for a Crusade to drive the Muslim occupiers out.

The Pope actually sold his proposed military campaign as a counterattack, pointing out that it was the Muslims who had invaded and seized the land from Christians in the first place. Never mind the fact that this counterattack had been delayed by about 400 years; Christians were told that they would be rightfully retaking land that had been stolen from them. As the Pope presented it, the reasons for the Crusade were twofold.

First and foremost, the Pope was answering a distress call from his Christian brothers in the East. The remaining segment of the Eastern Roman Empire, which consisted of Greece, most of Anatolia (modern-day Turkey), and large parts of the Balkans, was on life support. In the face of renewed Muslim aggression, it was teetering on the verge of collapse. Now known as the Byzantine Empire, this Greek-speaking relic of Rome's former glory was being threatened with utter annihilation by encroaching Islamic armies. The Pope hoped to prevent this by raising an army to defend the Byzantines—and alongside this goal, he also floated the idea of reclaiming the Holy Land. It was this complicated backdrop that led to the siege and reconquest of Jerusalem by Christian armies in 1099.

So where in this complex tapestry of conquest, religion, and political intrigue do the Freemasons come in? Some say that nascent Freemasonry arrived on the shoulders of a special order of crusading knights who called themselves the Knights Templar. This band of warriors came to prominence shortly after the Christian takeover of Jerusalem, spurred by the need to protect the thousands of Christian pilgrims from Europe who were soon streaming into the city to see the land of Christ.

Because then as now, the Middle East could be a dangerous place. Most of these pilgrims were not fighters—many were not even armed—and as such they made easy targets for thieves and revengeful Muslims alike. An armed escort of knights was deemed necessary to protect these spiritual seekers from the very real threat of physical harm, and the Templars were created for this express purpose.

Founded by a French knight named Hugues de Payens in 1119, the Templars were to be the perfect blend of spiritual and physical warriors. These men were basically to be an order of fighting monks who would risk life and limb to protect their fellow Christians. The name Templar is derived from the Temple Mount of Jerusalem—the site of the old Jewish Temple—which the young order of knights was given as their headquarters. (Why this newly established group was given such a prime piece of religious real estate upon which to set up shop has never been fully explained.) "Knights Templar" is actually a shortened version of their official title, which was the "Poor Knights of Christ and the Temple of Solomon". The biblical temple builder Solomon was an important figure for the Templars—and as we will see, Solomon is important to the Freemasons as well.

It has long been rumored that the Templars received a great secret when they took up residence in the Temple Mount. What the secret was isn't exactly clear, though—theories include everything from Solomon's treasure hoard to secret extra-biblical texts, and even the head of John the Baptist and the Holy Grail. It is perhaps due to the long history of such claims of miraculous finds that the military campaigns of the Crusades have become so conflated with treasure hunting.

But whatever secret treasure the Templars may have found, their primary mission was indeed a military one. They served as an elite strike force at the front lines of numerous engagements against Islamic revanchists. Ironically, as their esteem as protectors and guardians of the Holy Land grew, the "Poor Knights of Christ" began to become rather wealthy. Within a few decades the rich men of Europe were enthusiastically donating to their cause, giving the Knights a reliable source of income.

Not only that, the European upper class essentially began to use these trusted knights of Solomon's Temple as a kind of rudimentary banking system. They would temporarily hand over their assets to the order for safekeeping as they traveled to the Holy Land. These deposits soon added up to a large sum of money, and some believe that it is this more than anything that led to the Templars' eventual downfall. For the Templars were now powerful not only militarily; they had also become the financial masters of the European nobility. The leverage that this gave them over the kings and queens of Europe brought with it great resentment.

This resentment finally came to a head on the unlucky day of Friday the 13th of October in the year 1307. It was on that day that the Templars' French headquarters was stormed on express orders of Pope Clement V and King Philip IV of France. The official reason was charges of heresy, but considering the large amount of money that Philip owed to the Templars, it is easy to assume that his primary motive was a financial one.

The arrested Templars were sent to French dungeons and subjected to excruciating torture until many of them confessed to crimes they had most likely never even thought of—let alone committed. And whether they confessed to the charges or not, they were all eventually burned at the stake.

Pope Clement V, under continued pressure from Philip, disbanded the Knights Templar altogether five years later in 1312. The plotting of the Pope and the French King did not ensnare all of the Templars, however, and many managed to escape the dragnet that had been laid for them. So where did these survivors go? And just what became of them? Since most of Europe was now against them, they were forced to pick a nation still far enough off the beaten path to serve as their refuge—Scotland.

Scotland was so far removed from the affairs of its European counterparts—and even neighboring England—that when the Vatican issued orders to round up the remaining Templars, the Scots paid no attention whatsoever. Those involved in the manhunt for the outlawed Templars found that the trail grew cold after they fled to Scotland. And it is in the footsteps of these fleeing Templars that we find the first whisperings of the institution we now call Freemasonry.

It is no coincidence that many of the grand lodges of Freemasonry are called "Scottish Rite" cathedrals. It all goes back to the Knights Templar and their last refuge. Because almost as soon as the Templars disappeared into Scotland, the roots of Freemasonry began to emerge.

Freemasonry Officially Begins

The Freemasons officially revealed themselves to the world on June 24, 1717, when their first grand lodge opened in Britain. On this Saint John's Day, four previous gathering spots—all local taverns—pooled their resources to create one grand lodge in which they could all meet. This first grand lodge officially became a "regulatory body" in 1721. And as the typical conspiracy narrative would have you believe, in the centuries since that great coming out party, the Masons have always had their finger on one manner of intrigue or another.

With famous members such as George Washington and Benjamin Franklin, it has been said that the very founding of the United States of America was a plot hatched in a Freemason lodge. When France erupted in revolution a few years later, the finger was pointed at the Freemasons once again. But is there any truth in any of these claims? Well—the one country where Masonic influence would be the hardest to deny would indeed be the United States of America.

It is true that many of the Founding Fathers were Freemasons, and a trip to the national capital will reveal all manner of Masonic regalia on display. From the Washington Monument all the way to the design of the Pentagon, the Masonic square and compass have been put to good use. George Washington, who is probably the most famous of Freemasons, joined the craft in 1753 when he was 21 years old. He later led America to independence as a revolutionary general before becoming the very first president of the fledgling republic.

This republic was still fractured from the war, however, and the very loosely written Articles of Confederation drafted in 1777 weren't nearly enough to keep the individual states from splitting off and going their separate ways. A constitutional convention was accordingly held to resolve differences and create a unified government. The delegates to this convention were all from different backgrounds and walks of life, but often enough the one thing that held them together was their mutual participation in Freemasonry. For better or worse, this was a tie that helped bind them together even as they sought to tie up the loose ends of the nation.

However, the purpose of this book is not to examine these historical connections. Our focus here is to uncover modern Freemasonry. The modern Freemasonry of the last 100 years has attempted to shed some of the intrigue of its past with a friendlier gentleman's club type atmosphere. Whole new charters have been written for modern-day Freemasons to teach them how to be more open and congenial in order to attract new members.

But at the very same time, it is Freemasonry's last century that seems to hold the most drama and intrigue. Even as the Masons are attempting to put a fresh face on an old craft, as we will discover in the next few chapters of this book, there is still more than enough mystery to go around.

Freemasonry during World War One and its Aftermath

As the 20th century arrived, Masonic leadership was contemplating an expansion of the Masonic ideal on the world stage. At a Masonic convention in Paris in 1900, it was decided that the time was ripe for the implementation of a truly international Masonic order. This idea floated about French, British, and American Masonic lodges for the next couple of years without much action being taken. Then, in 1903, a former Grand Master from Switzerland, Edouard Quartier-la Tente, decided to make the scheme his own personal pet project.

It is interesting to note that just as the Masons were attempting to achieve international solidarity, the international climate of the world at large was beginning to unravel. The imperialism of powerful nations such as Britain, France, Germany, Russia, Japan and the United States was setting the stage for powerful collisions in their respective spheres of self-interest.

It could be argued that the first salvo of what would become World War One was fired against Russia by the Japanese in 1905.And when Japan defeated this once great Imperial power, it was proof that the old-world order could indeed be changed.

Conspiracy theorists who see a secret society behind the scenes of every political intrigue can find links to the Freemasons in every changing breeze of history, but most of this is mere conjecture. But in 1914, when the outbreak of World War One was all but assured, the spark that lit the fuse was indeed struck by a secret society—a group who called themselves the Black Hand. This secret cabal instructed a team of young Serbs to assassinate a group of visiting foreign dignitaries in Sarajevo, Bosnia. They succeeded in killing Archduke Franz Ferdinand of Austria and his wife, and the Austro-Hungarian Empire soon declared war on Serbia. This prompted Serbia's ally Russia to declare war on Austria-Hungary. And then, to make an incredibly long and complicated story short, due to a myriad of entangled alliances, practically all of the globe's great powers declared war on one another and were soon locked in a protracted struggle. This domino-effect downward spiral of worldwide conflict started with one lone terrorist associated with a secret society.

But who were the Black Hand? Wouldn't it be idle speculation to suggest that a group of Slavic radicals had any links to Freemasonry? Not so—if you were to ask the assassin himself. The very man who gunned down Archduke Franz Ferdinand, Serbian nationalist Gavrilo Princip, testified that he did so at the instigation of the Freemasons. He stated that one of his handlers, a man named Cigonovich who was a Freemason himself, had informed him that the Archduke had been condemned to death by a Freemason lodge. The lodge that had allegedly delivered this death sentence was none other than the Grand Orient de France in Paris.

According to Princip's testimony, he was a hit man hired by the Freemasons, who had already made the Archduke a marked man for a Mafia-style hit. Many have since denied these claims of a Masonic connection to the lead up to World War One as nothing but the fantastical imaginings of a deranged assassin. But you do have to ask yourself, why would a man, already convicted, with nothing left to lose lie? Princip died in prison, and he went to his grave stating that the Freemasons were behind the crime that he carried out.

You also have to wonder if it was coincidence that the Freemasons proved to be crucial in rebuilding the shattered institutions of the post-war world. After the war, US President Woodrow Wilson led the way in establishing an international body to handle future disputes. Known as the League of Nations, this short-lived precursor to the United Nations was fleshed out by Wilson's close adviser "Colonel" Edward M. House, who was a 33rd degree Grand Lodge Freemason. The organization was founded on April 28, 1919, and people have speculated about possible Masonic infiltration ever since. Such misgivings aside, the League of Nations began operations on January 10, 1920, with the stated objective of ending all wars.

This aim proved to be a tough pill to swallow for Italian dictator Benito Mussolini after he forced his way to power in 1922. Mussolini initially had many friends and associates who were Freemasons, but after he and his Blackshirts marched on Rome and consolidated their power, it wasn't long before Mussolini became deeply suspicious of Italian Freemasonry. His campaign against the Masons began with strict restrictions upon the press (of which many high-ranking Freemasons were a part). Masons who pushed back against the stranglehold that Mussolini had placed upon them became direct targets.

Soon, Il Duce had all of the major Masonic lodges in Italy shut down. In 1925 Mussolini famously remarked in an interview that Italian Freemasonry was a political organization that was subservient to the Grand Orient de France—the same massive Masonic lodge allegedly behind the assassination of Archduke Franz Ferdinand. Mussolini apparently believed that no Freemason in Italy could possibly be loyal to him, since they all took orders from this French lodge.

Shortly after giving this interview, Mussolini ordered the complete destruction of all Italian institutions remotely associated with the Masons. The brutal dictator declared, "Masonry must be destroyed and Freemasons should have no right to citizenship in Italy. To reach this end all means are good, from the club to the gun, from the breaking of windows to the purifying fire—the Freemasons must be ostracized—their very life must be made impossible."

The only one to stand up against this onslaught was Grand Master Domizo Torrigiani of the Grande Oriente d'Italia—the lodge that had been the center of Italian Freemasonry. After having his lodge forcibly shutdown, Grand Master Torrigiani challenged Mussolini by demanding that democratic principles be respected. Mussolini responded by having Torrigiani exiled to the remote Mediterranean island of Lipari, where he would die in obscurity.

All of this was certainly a slap in the face to the black-shirted Freemasons who had helped dear old Benito gain power in the first place. Shortly after ousting Torrigiani, Mussolini began to target lesser-known Freemasons and their associates. His fascist thugs forced their way into homes, ransacking the residences, terrorizing those unlucky enough to be found inside, and arresting and killing many in the process. The victims of this latest wave of persecution included another Grand Master, Raol Palermo, who was detained and eventually executed.

But perhaps the most famous Freemason that Benito Mussolini targeted was none other than Aleister Crowley. I know some may raise their eyebrows to see the dark British mage Aleister Crowley being labeled a Freemason, but in truth, there probably wasn't a secret society that Crowley *wasn't* a part of. If it was secret, mysterious and set apart from mainstream society, Aleister Crowley was sure to be a card-carrying member. And the Freemasons were no exception. In fact, if you study Crowley's teachings, the symbolism he employed, and even his dress, you can tell that much of what he used was either directly or indirectly borrowed from Freemasonry. Even though officials of Freemasonry endlessly deny that Crowley ever had any access to their lodges, the influence is very obvious. Crowley himself claimed to have been initiated by a man named Don Jesus Medina during a visit to a lodge in Mexico City. (It is perhaps rather ironic that Crowley, the man known as the

"Wickedest Man in the World", claimed to have joined the Freemasons under the auspices of a man carrying the name of Jesus.)

Whatever the case may be, Mussolini for one—after barring all Freemasons from Italian society—wasn't going to take any chances with Mr. Crowley. So, shortly after declaring Crowley to be much more wicked than he was, Mussolini had him driven out of his Abbey of Thelema—the occultist sanctuary he had built for himself on the island of Sicily. Crowley then disappeared from the Masonic milieu, but future Freemasons have been haunted by his presence ever since.

It is important to reiterate that modern-day Freemasons vehemently deny that Crowley was ever a member. And they do so for good reason. In the official Freemason charter, a good reputation and good moral character are prerequisites for membership. Someone like Crowley, who was known for conducting ritual orgies and sacrificing cats (and perhaps even people), could hardly be deemed an upstanding citizen by anyone's standard. But the fact that Crowley so frequently ripped off and coopted the secret rituals and symbols of Freemasonry for his own nefarious purposes is a clear indication that he was at least present at more than a few lodge meetings.

Freemasons, Fascism, and Communism

The aim of this book is to provide a fairly straightforward, chronological history of Freemasonry and the world events that it has allegedly been a part of and/or been shaped by. For this reason, we've expressly avoided bobbing and weaving from one date to another. We want to give you as clear of a timeline as possible, without any unnecessary complications.

Having said that, even though this chapter does pick up chronologically where the previous one left off—in the early 1920s—a little background is necessary. The rise of fascism and communism after World War One had some very complicated repercussions for the world at large and the world of Freemasonry in particular, and this requires a little bit of digging further into the past to understand just how these things came to be. But for the sake of chronological continuity, we will keep it brief.

First of all, the idea of communism as we know it originated in the mind of the 19th century writer and philosopher Karl Marx. Marx was not himself a Freemason (although it has been alleged that he had connections to the lodge in England, where he lived out most of his life). However, many of his followers were Masons, and the communist ideology he espoused would cross paths with Freemasonry quite a few times in the late 19th and early 20th centuries.

The biggest communist revolution occurred in Russia in 1917. The level of Masonic involvement in the Russian Revolution has long been debated. It is true that Freemasonry was rather widespread in Russian civic life in the early 20th century. The Freemasons were an intellectual bastion in Imperial Russia. Their lodges were places where otherwise oppressed Russians could openly voice their criticism of the Russian government.

It is interesting to note that the stated charter of Freemasonry today dictates that politics is not an allowable topic of discourse at Masonic meetings. This outward ban on speaking up on anything political was most likely put in to allay governments' fears about these secret gatherings. But if you believe the words of Alexander Kerensky, the man who led the initial revolution and briefly presided over a new Russian federal government before the communist takeover, the Freemasons were open agitators against the crown.

The Masons were allegedly fomenting revolution by encouraging peasants to go on strike for "bread and land". Others have made the claim that Kerensky himself was a Freemason, and allegedly even a Grand Master at a Russian lodge in 1916. But if conspiracy theorists wish to implicate Russian communists as

Freemasons, it would stand to reason that Grand Master Kerensky would have stayed in power. Obviously, this was not the case; Kerensky and the provisional government he headed were quite literally run out of town when the Bolsheviks took over the apparatus of the state.

Nevertheless, the idea that leading communists were Freemasons would continue to be bandied about in the following years. A few hundred miles to the east, in Austria, a young artist and military veteran named Adolf Hitler spent much of the 1920s virulently stating this case. He usually claimed that the communists were all part of either a Masonic or Jewish international cabal; when he felt the urge, he would claim it was a combination of both.

In his 1925 book *Mein Kampf* (*My Struggle*), Hitler devoted whole chapters to the disparagement of Freemasonry. He accused Masons—with the help of the Jews, of course—of attempting to take over all aspects of German society and conniving to steer the nation into the eager hands of the communists. Once Hitler came to power, he made it official; the Nazi party's handbook states that "The natural hostility of the peasant against the Jews, and his hostility against the Freemason as a servant of the Jew, must be worked up to a frenzy."

Hitler's diabolical ranting and ravings have of course been discredited, and no evidence has been found that the Freemasons were ever part of any sinister collectivist plot. Nevertheless, when Hitler was elected as Reich Chancellor in January of 1933, the Nazis rapidly went forward with their plans to shut down the Freemasons. The push to move the Freemasons out of Nazi Germany began with a stern warning given to the Grand Master of the Grand Lodge of Germany on

April 7, 1933, by Hitler's number-one loyal stooge Hermann Goering.

Despite the inhospitable nature of his errand, it is said that Goering was at least polite enough to say "please" when he asked the Grand Master to leave. The Nazis' manners didn't last for long, however, and soon they were rooting out whatever Freemasons remained by absolute brute force. Freemasonry itself was officially banned in 1934, making anyone who wore the Masonic apron automatically an enemy of the state. All throughout World War Two, the authorities in Nazi Germany systematically persecuted any Freemasons unlucky enough to be found inside the territory of the Third Reich. Tragically, many who could not escape ended up as fodder for the concentration camps.

It is estimated that as many as 100,000 Freemasons were killed in the Holocaust. Many of them ended up in the horrific facility known as Buchenwald, where they were at the mercy of the so-called Hangman of Buchenwald—Martin Sommer. This depraved Nazi was rather fond of hanging Freemasons (along with other inmates) up in the trees of the nearby woods, and due to the cries of the dying men dangling from them, the locals dubbed the grove the "Singing Forest of Buchenwald". Here the destroyed bodies of Freemasons, along with Jews, homosexuals, Jehovah's Witnesses, Gypsies, communists, and anyone else the Nazis deemed a threat to the state were hung from the branches.

But the saddest sight for many inmates was the tree that the famed German poet Goethe was said to have sat under during his heyday in the 1700s. This tree, which had been preserved and revered long before the Nazis decided to build a hellish detention center nearby, came to represent a twisted mockery of Germany's more enlightened past. It was high literature and art in the face of the dreadfully degraded reality of the concentration camps. Strangely, the Nazis had actually chosen Goethe as their anti-Freemasonry poster child, saying that this hero of German culture had been against the Masons. Even for the Nazi high command, this was an extremely bizarre thing to do, since Goethe had actually been a Freemason himself!

Along with the oppression dished out by the Axis powers under Benito Mussolini and Adolf Hitler, Freemasons had yet another totalitarian fascist dictator to fear in the form of General Francisco Franco of Spain. Franco seized power in 1936, sparking the Spanish Civil War. The claim that he was freeing Spain from communism and Freemasonry was literally part of this man's war cry, and any Freemason taken prisoner by the fascists was immediately executed.

But Franco was not satisfied with merely eliminating Masonic POWs, and he eventually decided to become even more proactive in his persecution of Freemasonry. In March of 1940, he set up his own modern-day version of the Spanish inquisition, the Tribunal for the Suppression of Masonry. Accompanying legislation not only made it a criminal offense to be a Freemason but also made it possible to punish a Mason's relatives. Franco's fascist regime was now able to rip entire families apart simply for their ties to Freemasonry.

Even Franco had to make exceptions in his brutality from time to time, however, as was the case when a couple of his own generals were found to be Freemasons. Although these men were forced to renounce their Masonic membership, they were ultimately spared punishment because Franco needed them on the field of battle during the ongoing Civil War. In the end, Franco won that war, and just as importantly he managed to keep his country out of the larger conflict of World War Two. Unlike its fascist counterparts of Germany, Italy, and Japan,

Franco's Spain was able to survive the conflagration intact, and when the smoke cleared he found himself to be the last fascist standing.

His hatred of Freemasons survived the war as well. Shortly after the Allied victory, Franco began to pen a series of anti-Masonic articles under the pseudonym of J. Boor. These articles were eventually compiled into an anthology called *Masoneria* which was published on May 3, 1951. In this book, Franco blamed the Freemasons for destroying the Spanish Empire of old—and for just about every other problem or crisis the country had ever experienced. Freemasonry remained officially anathematized in Spain until Franco's death in 1975, when King Juan Carlos succeeded him and rolled back the ban.

Freemasons, fascism, and communism have had a long and complicated history, and Freemasons have been scapegoated for just about every societal ill you could ever imagine. Fascist totalitarian dictators lashed out with fear against what they could not control and tried to shut down the free spirit of the Freemason for good. But the resilient spirit of Masonry could not be chained down, locked up, or denied.

Freemasonry of 1950s America

The 1950s was in many ways America's heyday of unprecedented growth. After the victorious war, the American economy was booming. And even as the former superpower of the British Empire was falling apart, the US had risen to the top as the military hegemon of the world. It was also during the 1950s that American Freemasonry reached its zenith, with the majority of the world's Masons belonging to a lodge within the United States.

For many Americans today, the 50s symbolize the good old days, but in reality, those good old days were fraught with all kinds of difficulty. For one thing, the Cold War threat of nuclear annihilation was never far from anyone's mind. The Atomic Age had begun when the United States dropped the first nuclear bombs on Hiroshima and Nagasaki in Japan—on the orders of the Freemason President, Harry Truman.

The atomic bombing of Japan has always been highly controversial for a variety of reasons. Number one, the idea of detonating a nuclear bomb over a city full of civilians now strikes most people as overkill, to say the least; and number two, evidence has since surfaced that seems to clearly indicate that Japan was on the path to surrender before the bombs were dropped. The question, then, is why did Truman do it?

Some conspiracy theories paint a picture of a US president influenced by a diabolical branch of Freemasonry hell-bent on making an example to the world of the power wielded by the coming New World Order. Now, the "New World Order" has been bandied about in conspiratorial circles for quite some time, but just what does it mean? Is this something that some blogger somewhere simply made up? Well, if you would like some sort of tangible proof, just pull a dollar out of your billfold and flip it over to the backside. Now look under the pyramid. You will see the phrase "Novus Ordo Seclorum". What does that mean? It's Latin for "New World Order".

Just how it got there, and what it means, has been debated for decades—ever since 1935, when fellow Freemason FDR commissioned the design for the bill. One theory is that the pyramid, which is unfinished and sports an all-seeing Masonic eye, is an allegory for the Masons' unfinished business of creating a world government.

It wasn't long after the end of World War Two that nuclear weapons technology spread to the Soviet Union, creating a nuclear standoff dangerous enough to threaten the entire planet. Were Freemasons behind this unexpectedly rapid nuclear proliferation? There are some who would say they were. There are KGB reports that spies for the Soviet Union were indeed seeking membership in Masonic lodges in the United States.

The most famous of these alleged spies were Julius and Ethel Rosenberg, who were convicted of handing America's nuclear secrets over to the Russians in 1951. The Rosenbergs had also managed to seriously endanger the lives of hundreds of thousands of US troops in the Korean War through the release of sensitive data on the capabilities of the US Air Force. This gave the Soviets near air supremacy throughout much of this engagement.

But not all 50s Freemasons were in cahoots with the communists. And one Freemason who particularly wanted to prevent the expansion of communism was General Douglas MacArthur. MacArthur initially led UN forces in the war that broke out on the Korean peninsula in 1950. Following the amphibious invasion of Inchon, he managed to push the communist Korean fighters all the way back to the Chinese border. He then intended to take the fight to China itself, even advocating the use of nuclear weapons to effect the complete decimation of the People's Republic. Harry Truman ultimately overruled MacArthur, ordering him to stand down and removing him from leadership due to his defiant stance.

Nevertheless, MacArthur remained legendary in Japan, where after World War Two he had served as the supreme allied commander and built the new Japanese governing structure from scratch. He had also made sure that a few Masonic temples were built as well. As early as 1947, he had the fledgling provisional government of Japan open the door for Japanese citizens to start and join their own Masonic lodges. These included a new lodge at Yokosuka Naval Base, as well as three separate lodges that were established in Tokyo.

Even while MacArthur was building up his legacy in Japan, a senator named Joseph McCarthy was building up his infamy back home in America. He was officially hunting for communists, but Freemasons were on his radar as well—so much so that many felt the need to create splinter groups and factions outside of mainstream Freemasonry in order to keep McCarthyism from getting inside the lodge.

One such group was initiated by the exiled Polish politician and Freemason Jozef Retinger. The group first met at the Bilderberg Hotel on May 29, 1954. It was from the name of this initial meeting site that this secret cabal came to be known as the Bilderberg Group or more simply as the Bilderbergers.

Among other things, the group had a stated objective early on for pushing towards a European Union. The EU was still very much on the drawing board in the early 1950s, but the Bilderbergers would push on until their dream became a reality. In fact, the first direct precursor to the European Union, the European Community, was conceived by the Bilderbergers and made reality with the Treaty of Rome—that old capital of European Empire—in 1955.

For many conspiracy theorists, the creation of a united European super state is just the first stepping stone to creating a world government. Proponents of this theory vigorously claim that groups like the Freemasons and the Bilderbergers are actively taking part in the process after having made major inroads in the 1950s.

According to some, the plotting and scheming behind the scenes was not all political. Some of it was cultural. There have been claims that Bilderberg-backed Freemasonry became heavily involved with the music scene of the 1950s, sponsoring acts such as Elvis Presley in order to influence the culture of the nation. This is all just conjecture, of course, and has not been proven one way or the other. But as you can see, the happy, idyllic 50s were not all about *Leave it to Beaver* and Ovaltine; there were some people with nothing short of world domination on their minds.

Freemasonry and the Killing of Kennedys

The election of John F. Kennedy was an exciting time for many Americans. It seemed to be a time of great hope and optimism in which, as Kennedy himself described it, "the torch had been passed to a new generation of Americans". But it is alleged that there were many "powers that be" behind the scenes that did not much appreciate the fact that this torch had been passed at all. Those who wanted to maintain the status quo saw the dashing young President as a great threat to their hegemony.

Contrary to many of his associates (who just so happened to be high-ranking Freemasons), Kennedy wanted to deescalate the crisis that was developing in Vietnam. He was considering a removal of US troops by 1965. Obviously, this is not what occurred, and after Kennedy's death in 1963, the US became increasingly locked into the Vietnamese struggle. But while it is certainly true that Kennedy's foreign policy ran afoul of many powerful people in Washington, DC, is there any evidence that his death was part of a Masonic plot?

Admittedly, the links that conspiracy theorists point to are tenuous at best. First of all, they highlight the coincidences surrounding the place and time that Kennedy was killed. He was gunned down on November 22, 1963, as his motorcade traveled through Dealey Plaza in Dallas. The so-called circumstantial evidence linking this event to the Masons begins with the fact that Dealey Plaza was named for a Freemason called George Bannerman Dealey. The plaza was also home to a giant Masonic obelisk that stood directly over the site of Kennedy's murder. Just a coincidence for most, but some see more. And if you're up for another stretch of the imagination, it has also been pointed out that as soon as Kennedy landed in Texas, he was greeted by a group of school children singing the song "The Eyes of Texas"—which just so happened to be written by a Freemason!

Most of us would find such insinuations from such minor details to be absurd, but there are many hardcore conspiracy theorists who maintain that there is indeed a connection between the assassination of John F. Kennedy and Freemasonry. According to these theorists, the gunman who was arrested for the crime— Lee Harvey Oswald—was just a stooge chosen to take the fall for the greatest assassination in history. As Oswald famously told the press immediately after the shooting, he "was just a patsy".

Oswald unfortunately never had the chance to elaborate on this statement, because soon thereafter he too was gunned down— killed by nightclub owner and petty mobster Jack Ruby. Ruby stated at the time that his reason for marching into a police station (he just happened to know exactly where Oswald was being held) and shooting Oswald before he could stand trial was simply that he was consumed by anger and indignation at the man who had killed the president.

This petty crook and racketeering gangster, it turns out, was a very patriotic man; according to Ruby, he simply wished to avenge John F. Kennedy. But those who knew Ruby best found such assertions entirely laughable. District Attorney Jim Garrison, who investigated the case, summed up the absurdity of Ruby's claims of being caught up in a patriotic passion when he stated, "Jack Ruby had no strong political views of his own. He was just a hoodlum out for a buck."

Whoever was responsible for Kennedy's death, he was succeeded by a powerful Freemason named Lyndon Baines Johnson. It interesting to note that while Johnson claimed he was going to continue Kennedy's policies, when it came to Vietnam he ordered an immediate change of course. Just a few days after Kennedy's death, Johnson rattled off a memo to one of the top generals handling the situation in Southeast Asia, General Maxwell Taylor, telling him, "The more I look at it, the more it is clear to me that South Vietnam is our most important military area right now."

Shortly after this directive was issued, the still-controversial Gulf of Tonkin incident occurred. The American version is that US naval vessels engaged in sea battles with North Vietnamese ships. The Vietnamese have always maintained that the attack never occurred—the whole thing was made up merely as a pretense for war. If this is the case, it would certainly fit into the Freemasonry narrative of "order from chaos". This is a belief that the best way to achieve an objective is to first create a problem (such as imaginary boat attacks), then find a solution (war in Vietnam), so you can get what you really wanted in the first place

(US domination of Southeast Asia). According to some theorists, this is Freemasonry 101.

Whatever the truth may be, right at the same time America was getting dragged into a horrible quagmire in Vietnam, the Masons of England were celebrating a major milestone. 1967 was the 250th anniversary of the founding of the first grand lodge in 1717. A rally to commemorate the event was held in the Albert Hall lodge in London. Over 6,500 Masons from all over the world attended this gathering. A quarter of a millennium later, the place where it all began was still going strong.

In the States, meanwhile, the Kennedy conspiracy was getting even thicker after Jack Ruby passed away in prison. The world was shocked when a Dallas Deputy Sheriff named Al Maddox revealed that Jack Ruby had confided in him his belief that he had been injected with "cancer cells" shortly before his death. Maddox claimed that Ruby told him, "They injected me for a cold—but it was cancer cells". Ruby apparently believed that he had been tricked into taking a vaccination shot that contained some sort of carcinogenic contagion. At the time, Deputy Maddox had just thought that Ruby was being paranoid—but when he died just a few weeks later from an extremely aggressive, fast-growing cancer, he began to believe Ruby had been telling the truth.

But that wasn't all—Maddox also claimed that shortly before Ruby died, he had handed him a small scrap of paper on which was scrawled the message, "It's a conspiracy! If you keep your eyes open and your mouth shut, you're going to learn a lot!" Now, if Ruby really did deliver this cryptic note shortly before expiring, it's almost certain he wasn't speaking of a conspiracy over the chicken nuggets in the prison cafeteria. If Ruby really wrote these words, he was clearly indicating that the Kennedy assassination and his involvement in shooting the alleged assassin were part of a vast conspiracy.

And many conspiracy theorists believe that it wasn't enough to kill John F. Kennedy, his assassin, and his assassin's assassin. It was also necessary to kill his brother with a mind-controlled robot named Sirhan Sirhan. The man who bore this double-barreled appellation was a 24-year-old Palestinian national who seemingly just happened to wander into the Ambassador Hotel in Los Angeles where Robert Kennedy was giving a victory speech following the California primary during the 1968 election. After his big win, RFK seemed poised to get the Democratic nomination when Sirhan stumbled upon the scene and shot him dead.

The gunman was tackled and taken to the ground immediately after delivering those lethal shots—and then it was as if he had just woken up out of a dream. Alarmed at what was happening around him, the bewildered Sirhan claimed to have no knowledge of what had just transpired. It was as if he had been sleepwalking when he pulled the trigger. How can we account for such a thing?

Well, if you believe some conspiracy theorists, the explanation is obvious: Sirhan was programmed by a dark Masonic cabal. According to Sirhan's own memory—or what is left of it—he was merely in the area looking for a party to go to. The 24-year-old was apparently ready to have a night out on the town when he stumbled upon the Ambassador hotel where Kennedy was speaking. He hit the bar and had a few drinks. Sirhan claims that after he left the bar, he realized that he was too intoxicated to drive, so he went down to the hotel pantry to get himself some coffee so he could sober up.

Here he claims that he met a pleasant young woman who began to chat with him. They made random small talk as the nice lady helped Sirhan fix his coffee. But after taking one sip of that coffee, the next thing Sirhan knew he was being tackled to the ground and accused of killing Robert F. Kennedy, who was bleeding to death just a few feet away. To this very day, Sirhan Sirhan claims to have no knowledge of what happened between that first sip of coffee and the aftermath of the shooting. Was Sirhan drugged? Or, as many conspiracy theorists and anti-Masonic activists claim, was he somehow programmed and placed in a hypnotic trance so he would carry out the shooting? What happened between him, the nice lady in the pantry and that cup of coffee? Some say she was a CIA agent working in tandem with Freemasons.

As strange as this tale has become, it gets even stranger with the uncovering of a Russian KGB memo that seems to implicate President Johnson himself in the assassinations of both Kennedys! It is hard to believe that an American vice president would collude with others to have his president killed so he could step up to take his place, but this is exactly what the most extreme of the conspiracy theories hold. And since Johnson was a high-ranking—yep, you guessed it—Freemason at the time, he had plenty of connections to help the plot go forward without a hitch.

So, who really did kill the Kennedys? Have you ever heard the expression "a picture is worth a thousand words?" Because you can discuss the inner workings of conspiracy all day long, but this one photo of then vice-president Lyndon B. Johnson exchanging a curious wink with Congressman Albert Thomas seems to tell it all. Everyone else in the picture is grieving the loss of John F. Kennedy, yet Representative Thomas, LBJ, and even his wife Lady Bird somehow seem to be quietly congratulating themselves. Congratulating themselves on what?

This photo was taken immediately after LBJ was sworn in, and it was initially excluded from the records—most likely due to the unseemly effect created by the winking LBJ and smirking Lady Bird. For several decades, only the photo shown at the beginning of this chapter was known to the general public. When this image was finally uncovered, it created a firestorm of speculation.
So what really happened? Who was really behind the killing of the Kennedys? If anyone knows for sure, they must have taken an oath of secrecy—because they sure aren't talking.

Freemasonry and Organized Crime

Any Freemason will tell you that the order refuses to have anything at all to do with criminals. In fact, one of the main stipulations for membership is to have good moral character— meaning no criminal record. Yet there are a few tales of Freemasonry brushing up against the dark underbelly of organized crime. And nowhere has this been more the case than in the Masonic lodges of Italy. It seems that dealings between the organized crime syndicate known as the Sicilian Mafia and Italian Freemasonry can be traced back to the oppressive dictatorship of that anti-Masonic fascist Benito Mussolini.

Mussolini tried his best to root out and round up Freemasons and Mafia members alike during the 1920s and 1930s. Il Duce despised any organization that he couldn't control, and both Freemasons and the Mafia fit that bill. However, his oppression had the unintended side effect of driving the Freemasons and the Mafia together. The old adage "we must all hang together, or we shall all hang separately" was never more apt than during the reign of Mussolini. Realizing that they would both sink if they didn't render aid to each other whenever possible, the two persecuted groups began a vigorous collaboration against the Italian government. In all irony, in targeting the Mafia and Freemasonry for extermination, Mussolini simply made both groups stronger as they created a tight network of opposition against his best (worst) efforts—so tight, that even long after Mussolini was dead and gone, these bonds would remain.

The centerpiece for much of the discourse between Italian Freemasonry and the Mafia was the so-called P2 Lodge, which operated under the jurisdiction of the Grande Oriente d'Italia. This lodge was in official use from 1945 to 1976, but by the late 1970s its charter had been withdrawn. Why was the charter withdrawn? Well, apparently, after a man named Licio Gelli was appointed Grand Master, it was found that he had ties with Italian fascists. The fact that a group of Freemasons would appoint a fascist to lead them after fascism had nearly destroyed them decades before is full of incredible irony, but this is apparently what happened.

When the governing apparatus of the Grande Oriente discovered Gelli's background they were appalled enough to disavow the lodge and cut ties with them. This didn't stop Gelli, however, and even without support from Freemasonry's centralized bureaucracy, he continued to run the P2 Lodge as an unofficial, yet fully functional satellite of the mainstream Masons.

For the rest of the 1970s, Gelli was busy bending the lodge to his own will. He built close ties with local politicians, wealthy bankers, and members of the Catholic clergy, as well as news media and publishing companies. One of the most important figures from this influential cabal that Gelli cobbled together was Michel Sindona, a top financier for the Vatican. It was through Sindona that a powerful banker by the name of Roberto Calvi made the acquaintance of Gelli and the P2 Lodge in 1977.

Known as "God's banker", Roberto Calvi was the President of the Banco Ambrosiano in Milan. Banco Ambrosiano was a top shareholder of the papal bank. After joining forces with the P2 Lodge, Calvi began to establish a string of foreign shell companies on its behalf, including ten located in South America alone. These offshore companies were notorious for their money laundering and other decidedly unethical transactions. The papal bank directly contributed to this money laundering scheme by helping to fund Banco Ambrosiano.

But soon enough Italian banking authorities began to zero in on the operation. Calvi knew that his days as a free man were numbered—but did he also know that his days of being alive were drawing to an end as well? Before the police could even swoop in to arrest him, in the summer of 1981 Calvi was found dead, hanging from Blackfriars Bridge, a famous landmark in far-off London.

From the outset, the scene of the supposed suicide seemed oddly staged. Calvi hung from the bridge by a bright orange rope wrapped tightly around his throat. Lodged deep in his pockets, he had wads of cash amounting to over 10,000 dollars—and a couple of bricks. As well as the obscure symbolism of bricks in Masonry, it would later be discovered that the orange rope was none other than the "cable tow" used in Masonic rituals. (It is a standard Masonic initiation rite to tie this cord around the initiate's neck.)

While many would assume that this was a clear message that death lurks for those Masons who decide to leave the lodge, Freemasons themselves protest that this cord has nothing at all to do with death. Although it may look like a hangman's noose around the initiate's neck, it is actually meant to symbolize the fraternal cord that connects all Freemasons together. Even if there is an innocent explanation for the orange rope, though, the fact that Calvi was hung from Blackfriars Bridge, a well-known Masonic landmark, made the matter suspicious in some minds.

Of course, even if Calvi was murdered, it wasn't necessarily by the Masons. Some suspect that the Mafia was the real culprit in the killing and sought to frame the Masons by using Masonic paraphernalia and a Masonic backdrop. But there was no proof either way, and the case was eventually shelved as one of the 20th century's more bizarre mysteries. Then, in 1991, Roberto Calvi's son Carlo reopened the investigation by hiring a private investigator named Jeff Katz to look into his father's death.

Katz and a team of 30 other investigators spent much of the 1990s doggedly searching for answers. They managed to trace a trail to several notorious underworld figures in the process, and apparently they struck a nerve. Because it wasn't long into the investigation that one of the detectives, Luca Tescaroli, was sent a mysterious package containing black powder, two 12-volt batteries, and a message on a scrap of paper that warned, "This is an ultimatum. Stop."

It was obvious that someone, somewhere, did not want the investigation to continue—but it did. The investigators uncovered an intriguing clue when they came upon British police records of the murder of a petty thug named Sergio Vaccari just days after Calvi had turned up dead. At the time, police had had little reason to believe that these murders were connected. The Rosetta stone proved to be the Masonic papers that Sergio Vaccari was carrying.

A fellow Italian Freemason with many of the same underworld ties as Calvi dying in London at the same exact time—it seemed to be a coincidence worth following. Picking up on this lead, investigators found that Vaccari had recently been kicked out of the apartment he was renting. Just before giving him the boot, his landlord had offered him another unit. In fact, he had apparently given Vaccari two choices, and a seemingly satisfied Vaccari had picked the one he preferred.

After getting settled in, however, Vaccari had requested information about the other option that the landlord had available. That option just so happened to be an apartment in a building called Chelsea Cloisters—which is where Roberto Calvi was staying prior to his sudden death. Once this revelation came to light, the Katz team was able to find several more all-too-coincidental links between Roberto Calvi and Sergio Vaccari.

Was fellow Freemason Vaccari somehow behind the murder of Calvi? And was Vaccari in turn murdered to keep him from talking? Anyone who understood how the Sicilian Mafia worked knew that a two-bit thug like Vaccari wouldn't be able to operate without marching orders from mob boss Francesco Di Carlo. But when Di Carlo was finally made to answer the questions of these intrepid investigators, he did not supply them with a confession. Instead, he cryptically responded, "I was not the one who hanged Calvi. One day I may write the full story, but the real killers will never be brought to justice because they are being protected by the Italian state, [and] by members of the P2 Masonic Lodge."

And sure enough, when five suspects were put on trial in 2005 for their alleged connection to Calvi's death, they were all acquitted. It seemed that they had bucked the system and skated free due to their beneficial connections. This, of course, only seemed to verify what the old mob boss Francesco Di Carlo had said about the state and Freemasonry lending their protection to Calvi's murderers. Could it be true? Are Freemasons somehow above the law?

Well, the idea of Masonic immunity to justice was literally put on trial in 2004, not in Italy, but at a lodge in New York. Here the Masons were once again in the headlines for all the wrong reasons, due to a standard initiation ceremony that ended in the death of the initiate.

Freemasonry's rituals involve much dramatic playacting, such as blindfolding members, putting ropes around their necks, and—as was the case in this tragedy—putting guns to their heads. In this particular ceremony, the goal was to induce a state of fear and obedience in the new Mason. But despite the high anxiety, no one was supposed to get hurt. Naturally, an unloaded gun is supposed to be used in such a ceremony, but on this occasion the gun was fully loaded. It went off and struck the initiate, a 47-year-old man named William James, right in the face. James was dealt a mortal wound and died almost immediately after being shot.

The Mason conducting the ceremony, Albert Eid, apparently had two guns on him that day, one that was loaded and one that was not loaded, and according to his testimony, he simply chose the wrong gun. From the outset this seems to be a tragic accident, but there are of course those who claim that the death of William James was not so accidental after all. And not all of them are professional conspiracy theorists.

In this case, there are conflicting stories from among the Masons themselves. You would think that a clandestine brotherhood worth the name would look out for a wayward member, but when it came to Albert Eid, the Masons couldn't seem to be bothered. Immediately after the shooting, Carl Fitje, the Grand Master of New York State, went on the record to proclaim that Freemasons do not use guns in any of their ceremonies. So, what happened? Was Eid's lodge going rogue and making up their own unofficial initiation ceremonies?

Eid was charged with second degree manslaughter, to which he initially pled not guilty. He explained that the initiation ceremony was supposed to have him shoot blanks as the new initiate, James, sat blindfolded in a chair while another Mason struck cans with a stick. This was supposed to scare James into thinking he had been shot. Unfortunately, the blindfolded man really was shot, and he perished so rapidly thereafter that fear wasn't even a part of the equation.

Eventually, Eid cut a deal and pled guilty to criminally negligent homicide, receiving a sentence of five years' probation. It was an extremely light sentence for such a charge—so light, in fact, that it has engendered speculation that Eid's ties to Freemasonry helped him get off easy. Perhaps we will never know.

Freemasonry in the Age of Terror

Of course, conspiracy theories about the Masons (or anything else, for that matter) wouldn't be complete if we did not—in one way, shape, or form—bring up the events of 9/11. Innumerable theories have been launched in regard to that tragic day in the late summer of 2001. They range from secret government cabals, to astrology and numerology, and to all manner of other so-called "secret sources of knowledge".

But clamoring the loudest among these conspiracy theories is the idea that 9/11 was the effort of behind-the-scenes plotters from a secret society such as the Illuminati or the Freemasons who sought to use their age-old model for change: order out of chaos. As mentioned previously in this book, it had long been a theme of Freemasonry to create order from chaos. The idea is that you create a problem, then offer a solution, and thereby generate the change you wanted.

In the case of 9/11, the theory states that the attacks were carried out to create a problem which would be solved by the invasion of the Middle East, which would bring the plotters what they wanted—control of Middle Eastern oil. It's a fairly basic formula, and some may find it outright absurd (if not insulting) in the context of 9/11, but there are many who subscribe to just this theory. In fact, the current President of the United States, Donald Trump, is one of the leading proponents of the idea.

Thanks to his previous life as a civilian building contractor, Trump considers himself an expert on architecture, and he has long insisted that the two planes that hit the World Trade Center should not have been able to take down the twin towers. According to Trump, the Trade Center was one of the first buildings to have been "built from the outside" with a network of reinforced steel supports on the exterior of the structure. As President Trump describes it, "Most buildings are built with steel on the inside, around the elevator shafts. This one was built from the outside, which is the strongest structure you can have."

Yet Mr. Trump maintains, "it was almost like a can of soup" the way the hijacked planes easily sliced through the buildings. So how, then, does Trump (and others) explain the destruction of the World Trade Center? Many contend that since the impact of the planes wouldn't have been enough, bombs must also have been detonated to take down the buildings. While—to be clear—

there is absolutely no proof of this, this 9/11 theory remains very popular to this day.

Some have even asserted that it was a plot by Freemasons in tandem with elements of the government that strategically placed tactical nuclear weapons in the buildings to bring them down. Was this another case of Masonic "Ordo Ab Chao"—"Order out of Chaos"?

Well, before we even look down that rabbit hole, let's consider that this conspiracy theory does not take into account all of the brave men and women who lost their lives on that September day—and who just so happened to be Freemasons. Yes, many of the firefighters, police and other emergency personnel belonged to the Masonic order. But despite their self-sacrificing support during America's darkest hour, it remains difficult for Freemasonry to shake the specter of these conspiracy theories.

Ironically enough, these same theories were eventually picked up by the Islamic terrorists for their own use. This propaganda methodology was on full display during the ISIS takeover of Iraq in 2013. In the United States, President Barack Obama had just won reelection when the chaos of ISIS began to disrupt the Middle East. The emboldened terrorists were tearing through Syria and Iraq virtually unchecked, and they soon began to launch personal attacks against President Obama himself in which they accused him of conspiring with Freemasons.

An ISIS spokesperson at the time issued the following statement:

The slaves of secularism and agents of the Freemasons appealed to their Crusader master, the Black of Washington, to save them from assaults of the Knights of Khilafah, who have become very close to conquering their capital, and eradicating their malice from the land of Muslim Kurdistan. So, the dog of the

Romans [Obama] thrusted his Air Force into a new dilemma; and entered into a military pact with the agents of yesterday, the Kurds, to commit the same stupidity that he had not awakened to, even until now! And it seems that this submissive fool forgot or pretended to forget the quagmire of Iraq years ago, in which tens of thousands of crusaders were annihilated and tens of thousands of them were injured with permanent disabilities, not to mention the material losses and financial crises that nearly wiped the United States off the map!

As you can see, the conspiracy theories that have been expounded upon so much in the West have made their way all the way to the battlefields of the Middle East. Right alongside their racist remarks about Obama being the "Black of Washington", these Islamic extremists clearly labeled any American intervention against them as being nothing short of another Crusade—and linked it explicitly to Freemasonry.

The irony of this whole situation is about as rich as it could get. Just before ISIS called Obama a "Crusader master", the president had been attempting to downplay their atrocities by making erroneous moral equivalencies between the Crusades of 1099 AD and the bloodthirsty murder, rapine, and destruction of ISIS. After these oddly apologist remarks on the terror group's actions, Obama was then ridiculed by the very extremists he had attempted to downplay! But whatever names and labels the Muslim mafia known as ISIS wishes to hurl at Barack Obama, as far as anyone can tell, President Obama has never been a Freemason.

However, his Secretary of Defense, John Kerry, most certainly was. And it is interesting to note that just as the war in Iraq and Syria really began to heat up, John Kerry went on the record to state, "We will make order out of chaos." As we have seen throughout this book, this is one of Freemasonry's best-known slogans. It is the strategy that they have preached to be the most effective means to effect change in the world. Coincidence, maybe—but Kerry and Obama's foreign policy during the Obama administration's second term did indeed seem poised to dismantle the Middle East.

We will have to go deep into conspiracy-theory land for some of this stuff—but it goes a little something like this: Do you remember back in the 2016 presidential campaign when Donald Trump shocked the world with the seemingly absurd statement that "Obama founded ISIS?" To most (including yours truly) this seemed completely ridiculous. But if you believe the conspiracy theory that deep state actors with ties to Freemasonry (such as John Kerry) are actively working to dismantle the Middle East, the perspective on Trump's seemingly absurd statement begins to shift.

Because here it is claimed that the American CIA, directed by President Obama, did indeed arm rebels to use as mercenaries in clandestine missions in the Middle East. This would certainly not be without precedent; the CIA has been doing such things for decades. Just think back to the Cuban exiles who were armed and organized by the Kennedy administration to overthrow Fidel Castro back in the early 1960s. Now flash forward to the 1980s, when the Reagan administration used the CIA to arm Taliban fighters in Afghanistan after the invasion by Soviet Russia.

The CIA ended up utilizing a guerilla leader named Osama bin Laden. Yes, that's right—that Osama bin Laden. It's undeniable now that bin Laden was a CIA creation set in motion to fight off the Soviet Union. You can argue of course, that after bin Laden served his purpose in the Cold War he became a monster that got out of control. How could his CIA handlers have known that he would go rogue and create the terror group known as Al-Qaida? But whatever the outcome, bin Laden's operation was indeed at least initially funded by the CIA—and some say, by the Freemasons.

So, can the same exact thing be said for ISIS? Was it indeed an Obama-backed CIA/Freemason project that got out of control? Is that why Obama always downplays the mess that erupted under his watch? Because he and John Kerry and a hidden Freemasonry/CIA deep state cabal were the actual founders of the terror group? Is that why in his final presidential address, Obama famously referred to ISIS as simply being the "JV" team? Were they initially proxies of his and a whole cabal of Freemasons? This is just one of many conspiracy theories involving terrorism and Freemasonry.

The Freemasons of the Future

In recent years Freemasonry has attempted a kind of PR campaign in order to gain new members. Because the truth is, the Masons are dying off. The median age of current members is from 60 to 80 years old, and without a surge in new recruits, this means that there will be a sudden drop in membership in the near future. In fact, it is predicted that an estimated 100 lodges will be forced to shut down and every single year if this trend continues.

It is for this reason that current leadership is forced to look toward the future—today. There have been continual efforts to convince the millennial generation in particular that it's "cool" to be a Freemason. In their outreach to these younger potential members, social media campaigns have been initiated online and several new university lodges have been created on the ground—all in an effort to attract the youth.

Young people are becoming increasingly dependent on internet-based community connections, so in order to survive and remain financially viable, the Freemasons of the future will need to utilize communication technology to keep themselves relevant. It has also been determined that the future will have to be more open than the past. The days of dark meetings in windowless lodges are over, and now the Masons are attempting to be much more transparent.

As much of an oxymoron as it may seem at first glance, this secret society is now seeking more transparency! This has been deemed necessary in order to combat some of the more rampant rumors that have been circulating about the lodge. Masonic leadership feels that in order to get people to stop talking about the more extreme myths and legends of the craft, they need to get them talking about something else. They realize that the best way to kill the gossip is to confront it head on.

Now many lodges are doing away with many of their more mysterious traditions, rituals and rites of initiation in favor of more pancake dinners, card tournaments, and fish fries. The Freemasons are becoming more of a communal and charitable organization, and there are many who believe that their future lies in following the example of the Shriners.

The Shriners are an entirely charity-focused organization that is a direct offshoot of the Freemasons. Shriners successfully raise millions of dollars for several worthy causes every single year. They have even created their own "Shriners Hospitals" to take care of the sick. With all of the good will they have created, you would be hard pressed to find anyone launching any diabolical conspiracy theories against them. Shriners march in parades, wear funny hats, drive miniature cars, dress up as clowns, and help kids with cancer, and you are unlikely to find such charitable

givers and helpers of the community lumped in with the
Illuminati!

It is for this reason that many believe that Freemasonry as a
whole needs to take this example and become much more
community focused in order to survive in the future. In order to
remain viable, keep up their membership, and avoid some of the
more conspiratorial tales they have been plagued with in the
past, this secret society just might have to give up many of its
secrets.

Freemasons—Are they Truly Free?

One of the most famous initiation rites for new Freemasons is for them to lift up their pant leg in order to demonstrate that they do not have any shackles attached to the leg on display. This is meant to show symbolically that the prospective initiate is not shackled or chained down to anything in this life and is a free agent able to make his own decisions. But how free are the Freemasons? Some detractors who have left the group would answer, not very.

These disgruntled former members allege that the Freemasons are nothing more than a cult. In particular, many Christians have left the group because they found that its rituals went against their faith. Certain symbolism, and perhaps the fact that certain higher-ups are meant to be addressed as "worshipful masters", has rubbed Christian believers the wrong way. This conflict has been with the Masons from the very beginning; it was the reason the Catholic Church banned the group long ago.

But ideological differences aside, could Freemasonry be said to be a cultish group controlling its members? Secrecy is a form of control, and no doubt the fact that Masons are expected to take and keep certain oaths could be viewed as a cult form of discipline. But having said that, several members have left the Masons and divulged secrets. Whole books have now been written exposing just about every supposed secret the Freemasons ever had. None of these former members have been killed.

So even if spooky rituals are conducted insinuating physical harm to those who leave the group, for the modern Mason at least, these seem to be nothing more than empty threats—used more to set the mood than anything else. In the case of William

James, who lost his life during a Masonic ritual in 2004, there was certainly an aspect of intimidation in the initiation, but as the shooter Albert Eid explained, it was just a scare tactic and nothing more.

All the members were so horrified at what had happened that they quit to distance themselves from the lodge that conducted the fatal ceremony. If mainstream Masonry is this skittish about an accidental death, it would hardly seem likely that they would purposefully cause the deaths of those who choose to leave the craft. Nowadays the lodge has a revolving door, with members going in and out as they please. Freemasonry may be in decline, but at least its members are still free.

Further Reading and Reference

Now that we have brought this book to a close, let's take a look at the many resources that made it possible in the first place. Here you will find thoughts and theories from all sides of the aisle when it comes to the history, influence, and impact of Freemasonry. Feel free to look through them as much as you like.

***The Secret Societies Bible: The Definitive Guide to Mysterious Organizations*. Joel Levy**
This book is an exhaustive reference point for secret societies. They're all listed in alphabetical order, so not only will you find Freemasons under "F", you will also find chapters on the Knights Templar, the Rosicrucians, and the Chinese Triads. This gives you a better understanding of all secret societies and how they connect and intersect with Freemasonry. If you would like to have a bigger picture of how Freemasonry interacts with other shadowy groups, then you are going to need to read this book.

***The Freemasons in America: Inside the Secret Society*. H. Paul Jeffersons**
This book shines a spotlight on the influence of Freemasonry in America. There is perhaps no other place on the planet that has been influenced by Freemasonry as much as the United States of America. This book helps to highlight the connections that the very Founding Fathers of the US had with Freemasonry—and how this connection to the inner workings of the lodge has continued to this very day.

***Rule by Secrecy*. Jim Marrs**
The late great Jim Marrs was a kind of connoisseur of conspiracy, and in *Rule by Secrecy* he does not disappoint. He takes us down every possible conspiratorial path you could ever

imagine when it comes to the Freemasons. From their founding
shrouded in mystery to more modern scandals and events,
Marrs covers it all.

The Freemasons: A History of the World's Most Powerful Secret Society. Jasper Ridley

In this classic expose on Freemasonry, Ridley relays the rich and
complex tapestry that Freemasons have woven throughout
history. Ridley is an expert historian, so you can expect nothing
but the best from his report on Freemasonry.

A New Encyclopedia of Freemasonry. Arthur Edward Wate

This compendium of all things Freemasonry literally goes down
the list, rattling off every important aspect of the craft. From facts,
to symbols, to secret rites, this book is a convenient source of
information.

Freemasons for Dummies. Christopher Hodapp

This book is not like your typical book from the For Dummies
series. Written by a Past Master, Knight Templar, and
Freemason, this book covers all the information that is allowed to
leave the lodge doors. You won't find much in the way of
conspiracy theories and sensational stories here, but for a
practical guide into the everyday mundane life of Freemasonry,
this book has no equal.

Born in Blood: The Lost Secrets of Freemasonry. John J. Robinson

In his discourse on Freemasonry, John Robinson takes us down
the path of conspiracy and details what he alleges to be the
"secret" side of Freemasonry that the general public knows
nothing about. This book takes us through some of the most
riveting tales to have come out of the Masonic lodge. You can
learn a lot here about the sordid affair of the Vatican banker

Alberto Calvi, who met his end when he crossed paths with members of the Sicilian Mafia working out of a Masonic lodge.

***The Hidden Life in Freemasonry*. C.W. Leadbeater**
Coming straight from the mouth of a Freemason himself, this book takes us through some of the twists and turns of Freemasonry from an insider's perspective. Here we can get some great insight into the craft's everyday routine. It isn't full of all the sensationalism of extreme conspiracy theory, but it's a solid guide to how the lodge actually operates. So if you would like to learn something concrete about the Freemasons and leave the wildest conspiracy theories aside, this book is well worth putting on your bookshelf.

Also by Conrad Bauer

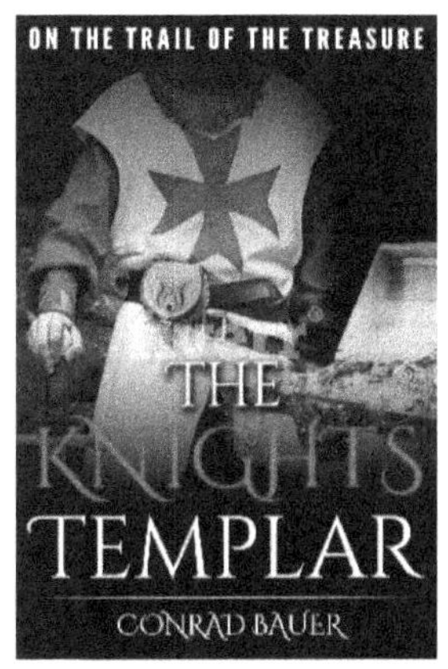

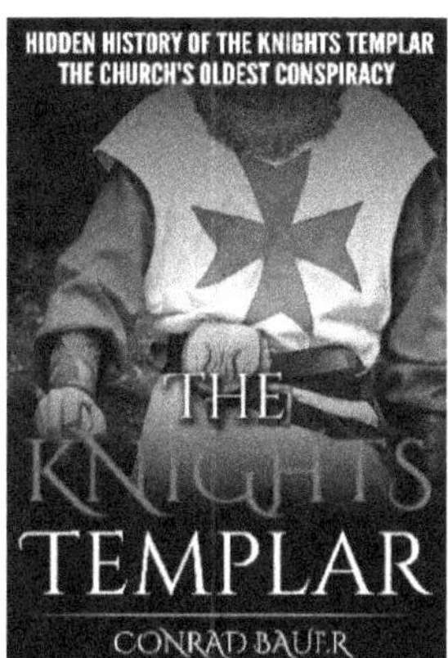

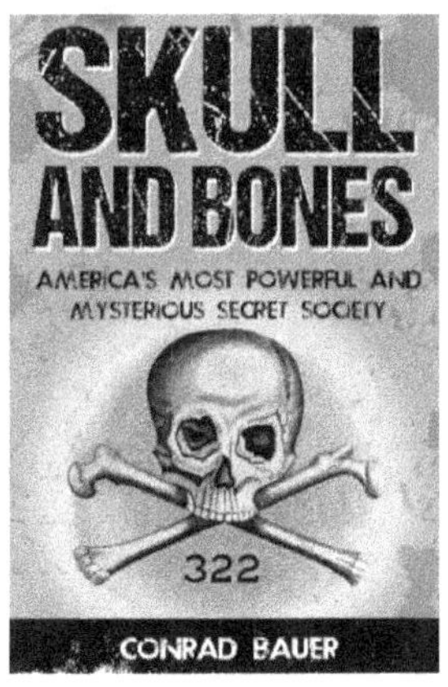

CONRAD BAUER
OPUS DEI
CATHOLICISM'S SECRET SECT
SECRET SOCIETIES

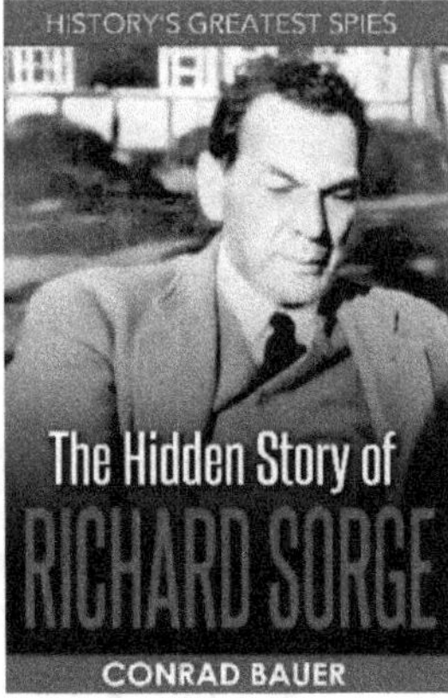
HISTORY'S GREATEST SPIES
The Hidden Story of
RICHARD SORGE
CONRAD BAUER

CONQUERORS OF THE WORLD
The VIKINGS
CONRAD BAUER

THE HIDDEN HISTORY OF THE CRUSADERS
AND THE CONSPIRACIES THAT FOLLOWED
The CRUSADES
CONRAD BAUER

NEAR DEATH Experiences
The Truth Revealed
CONRAD BAUER

NEAR DEATH Experiences
VOL-2
The Truth Revealed
CONRAD BAUER

THE STRANGE & UNEXPLAINED MYSTERIES OF THE WORLD
THE BERMUDA TRIANGLE
THE TRUTH REVEALED
CONRAD BAUER

SHERGAR
A True Crime Story of Kidnapping,
Racehorse, and Politics
CONRAD BAUER

DRACULA
THE ORIGINS OF THE MYTH
AND LEGEND
CONRAD BAUER